This Walker book
belongs to:

_____

_____

First U.S. edition 2019

Library of Congress Catalog Card Number pending
ISBN 978-1-5362-0536-7

18 19 20 21 22 23 CCP 10 9 8 7 6 5 4 3 2 1

Printed in Shenzhen, Guangdong, China

This book was typeset in Bookman and Avenir.
The illustrations were done in a variety of media.

Walker Books
a division of
Candlewick Press
99 Dover Street
Somerville, Massachusetts 02144
www.walkerbooksus.com

Flights of Fancy

Creative Inspiration from Ten Award-Winning Authors and Illustrators

Quentin Blake • Anne Fine • Michael Morpurgo

Jacqueline Wilson • Michael Rosen • Anthony Browne

Julia Donaldson • Malorie Blackman

Chris Riddell • Lauren Child

with an introduction by Anita Silvey

WALKER
BOOKS

CONTENTS

INTRODUCTION

Some of the world's best ideas occur in unusual situations. One of the great inspirations in the children's book world happened when two people went fishing. Not just any two people but British Poet Laureate Ted Hughes and Michael Morpurgo, author of *War Horse* (the basis of a play and a movie). As they enjoyed the day, they agreed that the UK needed some kind of national recognition for children's book writers. In 1999, with the help of Book Trust and Waterstones, the UK launched its Children's Laureateship initiative. In 2008, the success of the British program inspired Americans to establish their own National Ambassador for Young People's Literature. The Children's Laureates and the National Ambassadors spend time in their respective countries appearing on television, talking to the press, and visiting schools and libraries on behalf of children's books.

That fishing trip just keeps on giving. In celebration of twenty years of the program, the first ten Laureates prepared essays about their writing or illustrating processes. Although creativity usually happens in the empty spaces, many writers and artists find that they often need a little help—a prompt or an idea to get them started. In *Flights of Fancy*, some of Britain's most famous children's book creators—including Quentin Blake (illustrator of Roald Dahl's books), Anthony Browne (author-illustrator of *Gorilla*), Lauren Child (mastermind behind the Clarice Bean books), and Anne Fine (who envisioned the character immortalized by Robin Williams in the movie *Mrs. Doubtfire*)—share tantalizing suggestions that will get artists and writers started on a project.

Just like the ten imaginative people who wrote these essays, nothing about their ideas could be considered tired or shopworn. These are not your usual classroom assignments. Fifty-year veteran Quentin Blake sketches all kinds of fantastic vehicles and encourages young doodlers to get started on some of their own. Anthony Browne demonstrates how to play the Shape Game. In a search for the ideal bookplate, Anne Fine shares some of her favorite examples and shows how a bookplate can generate a short story. Michael Rosen takes one intriguing word, *bobble,* and transforms it into a poem. As Michael Morpurgo says: "I am a sponge: I soak up the world around me, then squeeze it out into my stories." Then he uses his experiences to weave a story about a librarian who saves books from burning. Other suggestions include taking a word for a walk, starting a notebook of favorite daydreams, and writing a short play based on a story.

These ideas have been designed for use at home, in classrooms, and in library programs. The book is a treasure trove for inexperienced teachers hunting for ideas and will enable veterans to move their writing and art prompts to a higher level. For children's book writers, illustrators, and enthusiasts, these essays explore the thought processes of some of the greatest masters of the craft.

Basically, anyone searching for creative inspiration will be grateful for this book. Don't hesitate. Pick it up along with a pen, pencil, and notebook—and get ready to find your best ideas yet.

Anita Silvey,
author of *100 Best Books for Children*

QUENTIN BLAKE

Children's Laureate 1999–2001

The Only Way to Travel

I have talked to children all around the world about words and pictures. Here I want to concentrate on the pictures, because I have been creating illustrations for books now for more than fifty years and it still continues to be exciting.

When illustrating someone else's text, the first thing you have to do is put yourself inside their story—you have to read it carefully and try to capture the atmosphere of the book, then get that into your drawings. If you think of Roald Dahl's *The Twits*, for instance, that story is very badly behaved, with lots of cruel jokes. It's like a caricature, not at all like real life.

Danny the Champion of the World, also by Roald Dahl, is much more realistic, and so I had to try to draw it as though the story were happening in front of me.

Generally illustrations belong to a story that exists already, but sometimes it's the other way around; I have drawn a lot of pictures for hospitals, and for that you have to imagine yourself in the situation of the patients and think about what drawings would be helpful for them to see.

Something that always fascinates me is deciding what to draw with. Most of the time I use watercolor paper and a scratchy pen, which I dip into a pot of black India ink. But I like to experiment with different tools: quills (mostly turkey feathers cut into a point, though I also have feathers from a swan, a crow, and even a vulture), reed pens, and brushes—especially for bigger pictures.

Recently, I painted pictures on a larger scale than I ever have before; it was for an exhibit I was asked to put on at the Jerwood Gallery in Hastings, England. I decided the exhibition would be called "The Only Way to Travel," which would give me the chance to make up all kinds of fantastic vehicles. The drawings were done on sheets of paper mounted on a wall, or lying on a table, or on the floor. Two were done on the spot in the Jerwood Gallery.

It's some of these pictures that you're about to see. They are still waiting for their story to be told: you might like to think one up for your favorite. Or

perhaps you'd rather invent a vehicle of your own—it can be anything you like, created using whatever pens, paints, and tools you choose!

These are splatter creatures and very excitable.

I like these Vehicles—I've drawn lots of them

Who is this bearded man?
(You probably know.)

Brave little dog

What is the aeroplane thinking?

Look! he says

Next stage in the
great adventure

My Home Library

I've always loved bookplates—those decorated labels you often see pasted in the front of very old books that say things like "From the library of Agnes Forsyth" or "*Ex Libris* George Harper."

It's still a treat to open a book in a thrift shop or a used bookstore and come across one. People from aristocratic families often used their family coat of arms for their bookplates—with shields and crowns and knights' helmets and so forth—along with a motto underneath, written along a slim pennant.

A lot of artists have designed their own in idle moments. My favorite one shows a child curled up like a cat in a chair, lost to the world and clearly deep in a book. (Her name was Tansy Pickett.) Inspired by my love of bookplates, I had an idea to help the sort of child I used to be, who picked up books wherever they could be found: in rummage sales, school swaps . . . anywhere. I wrote to sixty illustrators, begging them to design wonderful, fresh, and interesting bookplates that any child would love.

Everyone was generous enough to agree. Some designed them for babies or toddlers, some for elementary school readers, and some for teenage or grown-up readers. They're all sorts of shapes and sizes; some are in black and white, and some in color. (Of course, you can always print them out in black and white and color them yourself.) You can see all of them if you go to the website www.myhomelibrary.org. Choose the ones you want, and print as many as you like for free.

Maybe you want to give your baby brother a secondhand picture book you found in a thrift shop? Wonderful! Print a bookplate you know he'd like and paste it over the first owner's name. See? It looks as good as new.

Fed up with lending out your favorite books and not getting them back? Stick in Raymond Briggs's threatening book-plate before you hand it over, and you'll never have that problem again!

P.S. Remember not to paste a bookplate in a library book, as you're only borrowing it.

This Book Belongs to Me!

IMAGINE! You have a mom and a dad, four sisters, and a huge, hairy Saint Bernard dog. The house you live in is far too small for you all. But then your mom and dad see a house for sale on the other side of town—it's much, **much bigger**, but they can still afford to buy it.

Why? Because nobody else wants to live there. It's the **CREEPIEST** house you've ever seen: it's dark and gloomy, and almost every window looks out over a graveyard. A **GHOST** might want to live there. A **VAMPIRE** would probably love it. But back then I was only eight, and I hated the whole idea.

We'd only been in the house an hour or so before I noticed a door with a massive bolt across the top, higher than I could reach.

"So, what's in there?"

"Ah," said my mother. "Behind that door is the staircase down to the cellar."

"Can we see?"

"Not today—I'm too busy."

But by the end of the week, all our beds were sorted out, the carpets were down, and the pictures were up on the walls. I kept up the nagging, and in the end my father shot back the bolt and let my sisters and me follow him, very carefully, down the shaky wooden steps into the cellar.

It was chilly and damp and hung all over with ancient spiderwebs. The stone floor felt icy cold even through our sandals, and the walls were of the roughest brick. One filthy light bulb hung from the ceiling, casting weird, swaying shadows but giving out almost no light at all.

My youngest sister lost her nerve entirely, burst into tears, and ran back up the stairs. Two others clung to each another and hung back. My oldest sister and I crept forward, making sure we stayed behind my dad.

On the floor were a few rotting crates, overflowing with empty bottles coated with grime. A couple of broken stools lay beside them. A lamp had been knocked off a shelf and was in pieces next to a heap of gray rags.

"Nothing worth looking at down here," my dad said firmly.

I pointed. In the darkest corner was a huge old metal-banded trunk with a domed top and a brass lock—the sort of trunk in which a **pirate** might have kept his treasure.

"What's inside that?"

Even my busy father was curious. He fiddled with the lock till something shifted inside, and it sprang open. The lid creaked horribly as he lifted it, reminding us of every **GHOST** cartoon we'd ever seen.

"What is it? Is it a *body*?"

"Or a **SKELETON**?"

"Come closer and look."

No *body* and no **SKELETON**. The trunk was full of books and mildewed magazines. The musty smell that rose as we leaned over them made all of us sneeze. Everything in there must have been nearly a hundred years old.

I picked a book out, and its damp, rotting cover left weird green stains on my fingers. I opened it and saw, on the front page, a fancy decorated bookplate with the words:

Ex Libris

Viscount Molesworth

"What does *Ex Libris* mean?"

"It's Latin. It means the book is from his library," my dad explained.

"And what's a viscount?"

"An *aristocrat*. Not as important as a duke or marquess or earl, but more important than a baron. And no doubt quite rich, because books used to be really expensive."

I studied the bookplate. It was a patterned shield held up on either side by what looked like two fancy horses with wings.

"Griffins," my dad said. "They're imaginary beasts."

Underneath the griffins, a motto in Latin was written along a curled and wavy strip.

"What does that mean?"

My father carried the book over to underneath the swaying light. "I think it says, 'LOVE FOR MY COUNTRY WILL TRIUMPH.'"

One of my sisters picked out another book and opened it to find the very same bookplate inside. Then the same in another. And another.

"Why did he bother sticking labels in all his books?" she asked.

"People did it because they wanted anyone who borrowed them to be sure to give them back. But you wouldn't bother to design and print your own bookplates unless you were rich enough to have quite a big private library."

Oh, wouldn't you? I had no money, but I set to work that day to design my own personal bookplate. Frankly, I'm terrible at drawing: My rabbit looked all **wonky**. My cat looked seriously **weird**. My very ambitious stab at drawing a prince on a horse looked more like a chimpanzee on a four-legged barrel.

In the end, I gave up on the pictures and just wrote:

This book BELONGS to:
ME
YOU GIVE IT
BACK,
(OR) ELSE!!!

Not very friendly, but it did the trick—and it was the start of my own home library. Now you start yours.

MICHAEL MORPURGO

Children's Laureate 2003–2005

Find Your Own Voice

I have traveled far and wide telling my stories—and encouraging children like you to dream up stories of their own. The way I like to do this is to explain what works for me as a writer, in the hope that it might help you find your voice.

I am a sponge: I soak up the world around me, then squeeze it out into my stories. A sponge that stays dry is a sad sort of a sponge, no use to itself or others. It has no story to tell. The poet Ted Hughes once told me, when I was stuck writing *War Horse*, that I should never sit down and face the blank page without first having soaked myself in the story. Read around it, research it, find out all you can, immerse yourself—then the blank page will not be frightening.

It's what I have done ever since; I do not think I have ever written a story that did not grow from the seed-corn of some event that happened in my life, or in the lives of others, or in history. Some stories are grown from more than one seed-corn, like "I Believe in Unicorns"—the one you're about to read.

Like several of my fellow writers, I have come across so many librarians, as an invited author, reading to children who sit there cross-legged on the floor, covering the carpet from bookshelf to bookshelf. The librarian knows—and I know—that maybe for one of those children, to whom books have always been boring, life might suddenly be transformed. Maybe that child will love a story for the first time, and become a reader for life . . . or a writer. Librarians are the unsung heroes in all this.

Which is partly why I one day found myself writing the story you're about to read, about a librarian who was to become a hero. I also remembered an extraordinary story I heard in Russia about a librarian who rescued hundreds of books from his library when it was on fire. And I never forgot reading for the first time, when I was young, how in the 1930s, the Nazis in Germany had burned piles of books that they did not want to be read.

Sponges like me use all of our senses to the full, always keeping our antennae out. We take nothing for granted, are full of wonder and belief and doubt, and full of questions. So in a nutshell, here's some advice based on how this writer finds his voice for every story he writes:

- ✳ Once you have stumbled upon an idea that you feel might be the beginning of something, don't just try to get going. Dream it out in your mind's eye, till you know the people in your story, till the people and places become alive, till you know you can sit down and start writing—and finish too.
- ✳ Write the story down onto the page as fast as the words and ideas will flow. And once I'm on my second draft, I always read the story out loud. It comes alive then, and you know whether or not you have done well. So it continues chapter by chapter.
- ✳ I never abandon a story once begun. Nothing is more likely to knock your confidence the next time you try to start a story.

Anyway, young writer, you can ignore all this if you like and go your own way. You be the writer you want to be. Don't take any notice of me. You tell it your way!

I Believe in Unicorns

My name is Tomas Porec. I was seven years old when I first met the unicorn lady. I believed in unicorns then. I am nearly twenty now and because of her I still believe in unicorns.

⟨⟨⟩⟩

My little town, hidden deep in its own valley, was an ordinary place, pretty enough but ordinary. I know that now. But when I was seven, it was a place of magic and wonder to me. I fished in the stream below the church, tobogganed the slopes in winter, swam in the lake in the summer. On Sundays, my mother and father would take me on walks or on picnics, and I'd roll down the hills, over and over, and end up lying there on my back, giddy with joy, the world spinning above me.

I never did like school, though. It wasn't the school's fault, nor the teachers'. I just wanted to be outside all the time. As soon as school was over, it was back home for some bread and honey — then off to play. But one afternoon my mother had other ideas. She had to do some shopping in town, she said, and wanted me to go with her.

"I hate shopping," I told her.

"I know that, dear," she said. "That's why I'm taking you to the library. You can listen to stories for an hour or so. There's a new librarian, and she tells stories after school to any children who want to listen. Everyone says she's brilliant."

"But I don't want to listen," I protested.

My mother simply ignored all my pleas, took me firmly by the hand, and led me to the town square. She walked me up the steps into the library. "Be good," she said, and she was gone.

I could see there was an excited huddle of children gathered in one corner. Some of them were from my school, but they all looked a lot younger than me. I was just about to turn and walk away in disgust when I noticed they were all jostling one another, as if they were desperate to get a better look at something. I went a little closer. The children began to settle down on the carpet, and there, in the corner, I saw a unicorn! He was lying absolutely still, his feet tucked neatly under him. I could see now that he was made of carved wood and painted white, but he was so lifelike that if he'd gotten up and trotted off, I wouldn't have been at all surprised.

Beside the unicorn, and just as motionless, stood a lady with a smiling face, a bright flowery scarf around her shoulders. When her eyes found mine, her smile beckoned me to join them. Moments later, I found myself sitting on the floor with the others, watching her and waiting. She was patting the unicorn and smoothing his coat. She sat down on him then, but very carefully, as if he were real and she didn't want in any way to alarm him. I could feel expectation all around me.

"The unicorn story!" cried a little girl suddenly. "Tell us the unicorn story. Please."

The librarian began talking so softly that I had to lean forward to hear her. But I wanted to hear her, everyone did, because every word she spoke was meant and felt, and sounded true. The story was about how the last two magic unicorns alive on earth had arrived just too late to get on Noah's ark with all the other animals. The waters rose and rose around them until their hooves were covered, then their legs, then their backs, and so they had to swim. They swam for so long, and they swam so far, that in the end they turned into whales. They never lost their magical powers and they still kept their wonderful horns, which is why there are to this day whales with unicorn horns. They're called narwhals. And sometimes, when they've had enough of the sea and want to see children again, they swim up onto a beach and find their legs and become unicorns once more — magical unicorns.

After she had finished, no one spoke. It was as if we were all waking up from some dream we didn't want to leave.

There were more stories after this, then some poems too. And when she finished each one, all I wanted was more. "Now it's your turn," she said. "Who would like to tell us a story today?"

A hand went up. It was a small boy from my school, Milos with the sticky-up hair. "Can I tell a story, miss?" he asked. So, sitting on the unicorn, he told us his story. And one after another, the children wanted their turn on the magical unicorn. I longed to try myself, but I didn't dare. I was frightened of making a fool of myself, I think.

The hour flew by.

"What was it like?" my mother asked me on the way home.

"All right, I suppose," I said. But at school the next day, I told all my friends what it was really like, all about the unicorn lady — everyone called her that — and her amazing stories and the magical storytelling power of the unicorn.

They came along with me to the library that afternoon. Day after day, as word spread, the little group in the corner grew until there was a whole crowd of us. We would rush to the library now to get there first, to find a place close to the unicorn, close to the unicorn lady. Every story she told held us entranced. And each day I wanted so much to take my turn on the magical unicorn and tell a story, but I could never quite summon up the courage.

ONE AFTERNOON, the unicorn lady reached into her bag and took out a rather old and damaged-looking book, all charred at the edges. It was, she told us, her very own copy of *The Little Match Girl* by Hans Christian Andersen. That day I was sitting very close to the unicorn lady's feet, looking up at the book. "Why's it been burned?" I asked her.

"This is the most precious book I have, Tomas," she said. "When I was very little, I lived in another country. There were wicked people in my town who were frightened of the magic of stories and of the power of books, because stories make you think and dream; books make you want to ask questions. And they didn't want that. I was there with my father watching them burn a great pile of books, when suddenly my father ran forward and plucked a book out of the fire. The soldiers beat him with sticks, but he held on to the book and wouldn't let go. It was this book. It's my favorite book in all the world. Tomas, would you like to come and sit on the unicorn and read it to us?"

I had never been any good at reading out loud. I would always stutter over my consonants, worry over long words. But now, sitting on the magic unicorn, I heard my voice strong and loud. It was like singing a song. The words danced on the air and everyone listened.

◐ⅢⅢↄ

ONE SUMMER MORNING, early, war came to our valley and shattered our lives. Before that morning I had known little of war. I knew some of the men had gone to fight, but I wasn't sure what for. On television I had seen tanks shooting at houses and soldiers with guns running through the trees, but my mother always told me it was far away and I shouldn't worry.

I remember the moment. My mother had sent me out to open up the hen coop and feed them, when I looked up and saw a single plane come flying in low over the town. I watched as it circled once and came again. That was when the bombs began to fall, far away at first, then closer, closer. And suddenly my family was all running, running up into the woods. I was too frightened to cry.

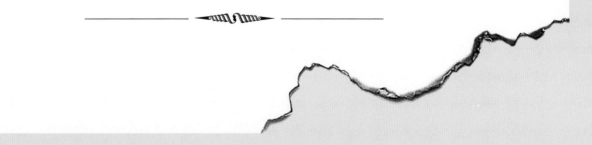

Hidden under the trees, we could see the tanks and soldiers moving through the streets, blasting and shooting as they went. A few hours later, after they had gone, we could hardly see the houses with all the smoke. We waited until we were sure the soldiers had all gone, and then we ran back home. We were luckier than many. Our house had not been damaged. It was soon obvious that the center of town had been hardest hit. Everyone seemed to be making their way there. I ran on ahead, praying that the library had not been bombed, that the unicorn lady and the unicorn were safe.

As I came into the square, I saw smoke rising from the roof of the library and flames licking out of the upper windows. We all saw the unicorn lady at the same moment. She was coming out of the library carrying the unicorn, staggering under its weight. I ran up the steps to help her. Between us, we set the unicorn down at the foot of the steps, and she sat down exhausted, racked with a fit of coughing. "The books," she breathed. "The books."

When she began to walk back up the steps, I followed her without thinking.

"No, Tomas," she said. "You stay here and look after the unicorn." Then she ran into the library, only to reappear moments later, her arms piled high with books. That was the moment the rescue began. People surged past me up the steps, my mother and father among them.

It wasn't long before a whole system was set up. We children made two chains across the square from the library to the café, and all the rescued books went from hand to hand, ending up in stacks on the floor of the café. The fire was burning ever more fiercely, the flames crackling, smoke billowing now from the roof. No fire engines came — we found out later the fire station had been hit. Still the books came out. Still the fire burned, and more and more people came to help, until the café was filled with books and we had to use the grocery shop next door.

The moment came when there were suddenly no more books to pass along and

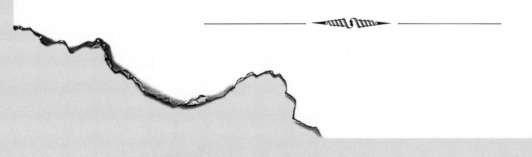

20

we wondered why. Then we saw everyone coming out of the library, and last of all the unicorn lady, helped by my father. They came slowly down the steps together, their faces smudged and blackened. The unicorn lady sat down heavily on the unicorn and looked up at the burning building.

"We did it, children," she said. "We saved all we could, didn't we? I'm sitting on the unicorn so any story I tell is true. We shall build our library up again just as it was. Meanwhile we shall look after the books. Every family can take home all the books they can manage and care for them. And when, in one year or two or three, we have our new library, then we shall all bring back our books, and we shall carry the magic unicorn inside and we shall all tell our stories again. All we have to do is to make sure this story comes true."

SO IT HAPPENED, just as the unicorn lady said it would. Like so many families in the town, we took home a wheelbarrow full of books and looked after them. Sure enough, the war ended and the library was rebuilt. It looked just the same as the old one, and we all brought our books back just as the unicorn lady had told it in her story.

The day the new library opened, because I had helped carry the unicorn out, I got to carry him back up the steps with the unicorn lady. The whole town was there, cheering and clapping, the flags flying, the band playing. It was the proudest and happiest day of my life.

Now, all these years later, we have peace in our valley. The unicorn lady is still the town librarian, still reading her stories to the children after school. As for me, I'm a writer now, a weaver of tales. And if from time to time I lose the thread of my story, I just go and sit on the magical unicorn and my story flows again.

So, I believe in unicorns. I believe in them absolutely.

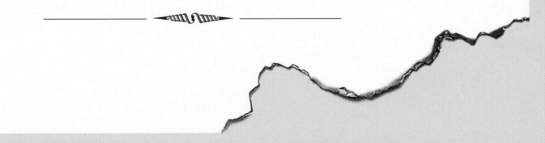

JACQUELINE WILSON

Children's Laureate 2005–2007

WHAT HAPPENS NEXT?

Do you like writing stories? Perhaps you love making things up and are never at a loss for ideas. Maybe you've already filled several notebooks with your own stories, or typed them out neatly on a computer. You don't need any help from me!

However, you might be someone who finds writing stories really hard work. Do you groan and make faces and stare at the blank page in front of you, without having a clue how to start? Do you get stuck after a couple of paragraphs, with no idea of how to get to the end of your story? Or maybe you've written three whole pages but it's in your biggest writing and your characters are just saying silly things to each other because you don't know what to do with them.

Don't worry! There are lots of ways of making writing stories fun. First of all, you need a plot. Something's got to happen. Try playing a "What If?" game.

Look around you:

What if there was a hurricane, and your house flew through the air to another land?

What if you went out your front door and a stray puppy rushed up to you and licked your knees?

What if your best friends at school suddenly started being horrid and ganged up on you?

Then write the story of what happens next!

It's easy to make up characters too—the people in your story. Decide whether you want to write about a girl, or a boy, or a horse, or a little green man from outer space. What do they look like? Are they funny, or scary, or sorry for themselves? What do they like doing most? What do they like to eat or drink? They'll soon start to seem real to you.

Do you want to write in a traditional, third-person way: "Lucy was thrilled with her new notebook." Or do you want to write in the first person, as if Lucy is talking to you directly: "Do you like my new notebook?"

I like writing this second way. I've written the following story as if Lucy is writing a vacation diary. Why don't you have a go at writing a story diary-style too?

THE WHITE HORSE

Saturday
o — o — o — o

Do you like my new notebook? The cover is bright blue with a white horse galloping across the sky.

I wanted to start writing in it right away on the car ride to the ocean, but Mom wouldn't let me in case I got carsick. So I just played with it instead, waving it up and down in the air.

"Look at my horse—it's **FLYING**!" I said.

"Horses can't fly," said Mark.

"This one can," I said, and I made the horse on my notebook fly around in the back of the car.

Dad braked sharply, and the notebook horse flew off course and collided with Mark.

"For goodness' sake!" said Mark, batting the notebook out of my hand.

The horse somersaulted through the air, flew over Mom's head, and landed on her lap.

"Hey, hey, stop clowning around in the back of the car," said Mom. "You know you shouldn't distract Dad when he's driving."

"Aren't we nearly there yet, Dad?" I asked. "You said we'd be there by lunchtime."

"It's not my fault there's this awful traffic jam. The world and his wife seem to be going on vacation today."

"The world, his wife, and his two children, Mark and Lucy," I said. "Mom, what shall I write in my lovely new notebook?"

"Why don't you keep a vacation diary?" said Mom.

So I am!

Sunday
– x – x

We're staying in a house halfway up a hill in the middle of the country. Mom and Dad have the big bedroom and Mark has the second biggest bedroom and I have a lovely little attic room with bluebells on the curtains and a cozy blue rug. If I stand at my bedroom window and stare hard, I can see the ocean glimmering in the distance.

That's not all I can see. There's another hill opposite our vacation house: it's covered with green grass like any other hill, but it's the most special hill in all the world because it's got a big picture scratched into the chalky rock. **It's a white chalk horse,** and I have the feeling it's winking at me!

It doesn't have wings like the horse on this notebook, but it's a splendid horse all the same. It's not quite as white, either, but that's not surprising because Mom says the chalk horse on the hill is hundreds of years old.

Mark's annoyed because he can't see it from his window. Mom and Dad can't see it from their window, either. I'm the only one who can see the horse.

I wish we could climb the hill and go right up to it, but the hill looks very steep and there are thick woods with nettles and bramble bushes all around—as if they're protecting the horse from intruders.

The horse doesn't have any eyes.

Monday
ⱳⱳⱳⱳ

We went to the beach yesterday evening and ate fish and chips sitting on the sand, and then went paddling in the ocean while the sky turned pink with the sunset. Today I wanted to try to walk to the horse, but we went to the beach again.

It was sunny and Mom made us a picnic, and we all went swimming. I can swim—Mark says I keep my foot on the bottom, but I don't.

(Not always.)

I said I didn't want to go to the beach today: I wanted to go on a white horse hunt. I was sure we could get through the woods—and **WHO CARED** if the nettles stung and the brambles scratched?

But when we tried, I cared quite a lot. We had to give up and go for another walk instead, and ended up having ice cream in the village there.

Tuesday

I say **good morning** to the horse when I wake up and **good night** when I go to bed. I know he doesn't have a real mouth, but I saved two sugar cubes from the tearoom we went to today. (I had carrot cake with lots of creamy frosting.) I held my hand out my window with the sugar cubes flat on my palm—that's the way you're supposed to feed horses.

Mark came into my room to borrow my flashlight. We both read in bed in the dark, but Mark's battery had run out.

"You're weird," he said, seeing what I was doing. "Do you really think he's going to come galloping down the hill to you just because you can't climb up to him?"

"He might," I said.

"You'd be scared stiff if he did. He'd be enormous, as big as this house," said Mark.

"I wouldn't be a bit scared," I said, though I hadn't actually thought the horse would be that big close up. "He's my friend."

"What's your friend's name, then? Chalky?" Mark suggested.

Chalky! As if. I'm going to find a marvelous name for my horse.

Moonbeam?

Silverlegs?

Starshine?

I can't decide.

Wednesday

I've found a wonderful name for my horse!

It poured rain all day: we couldn't go to the beach or out for a walk, so we stayed home. Dad made us pancakes for breakfast with maple syrup, then we went to the game room in the basement. (I wish we had one at home.)

We played Ping-Pong—I had three games with Mark. He won them all and said I was hopeless, but then we had the Family Ping-Pong Championships, Mark and Dad against Mom and me.

And guess what? **We WON!** Mom is brilliant at Ping-Pong: we made her a tiny gold trophy out of shiny yellow toffee wrappers.

After lunch (baked potatoes and beans), I started looking at the shelf of children's books in the game room. I couldn't find one about a horse. Mark looked at a book on Greek ~~with my~~ my~~thology~~ mythology. (Very difficult to spell!)

"Here, there's a magic white horse in this story," he said. "He's got great big wings and flies everywhere. He's called **Pegasus**."

"Then my horse on the hill is called Pegasus too!" I said.

"But your horse hasn't got any wings," said Mark.

"He might," I said. "Maybe he's just keeping them folded up for now."

Thursday

I went to bed after dark, so I couldn't see the horse, but I called out to him: "GOOD NIGHT, PEGASUS!"

It was still really stormy, but I'm sure I heard him call back to me—though Mark would have said it was the wind.

It was still and sunny when I woke up. When I ran to the window, there was my horse shining white in the sunlight —and I saw there was a shadow across his broad side. It looked just like a folded wing.

"Can you fly, Pegasus?" I called.

I saw the shadow on his side flicker—I really did.

We went to the beach and made a huge sandcastle with turrets and a moat. It was my job to run to the sea with a bucket to keep the moat filled with water. When I got tired, I lay on my back on a towel and watched the seagulls swooping overhead.

You can't see their feet when they're flying: I think they tuck them away neatly so they don't dangle and get in the way. I wondered how a flying horse would organize its legs. I tried to make a picture of the white horse in the sand, but I couldn't get his legs to go the right way.

"You and your horse," said Mom. "You'll miss him when we go home on Saturday."

"Perhaps he'll come with us, galloping along behind our car," I said.

I wish he could, but he wouldn't like it where we live. It's all apartment buildings and shopping centers—we haven't got any green hills anywhere.

Friday
o - o - o

Our last full day. We go home tomorrow. I wish-wish-wish we could stay: I'm going to miss my horse so much.

I had an apple after breakfast and took it upstairs with me. I held it out the window, and I'm absolutely positive Pegasus moved his head and pawed the ground. I know he did.

We tried to reach him today. Dad drove us to a lookout point on the other side of his hill, and we tried to hike to Pegasus from there. But there were more brambles and thicker nettles. I was wearing shorts, and now I have bright-pink itchy legs. Dad poured some water from his water bottle to help take the sting away.

"It's no use, Lucy, love," he said. "We can't reach him, even if I give you a piggyback ride. The hill is just too steep on both sides. I'm so sorry."

I cried a bit then, and Mark called me a baby, but when we got banana splits after lunch he gave me his cherry—even though it's his best bit too.

We spent all afternoon on the beach. I went swimming and managed six strokes without putting my foot down once! We had supper on the beach. Dad made a little fire and cooked sausages in a pan, and we had peaches for dessert and a big slice of chocolate cake.

When we got home, I stood at my window and stared toward my horse, wishing and wishing and wishing.

Saturday at six o'clock in the morning!

You'll never ever guess what! I woke up in the middle of the night, and I went and opened the window. The moon was very bright, so it was almost as light as day. But I couldn't see my horse! I rubbed my eyes and stared—where had he gone?

Then I heard galloping, getting louder and louder . . .

AND THERE HE WAS: MY WHITE HORSE, COMING FOR ME!

He soared over the tall hedge, then slowed to a gentle trot, delicately picking his way through the flowers until he was standing by my window, his huge head pressed against the glass. He had eyes now, big brown eyes with long lashes, staring straight at me.

I reached out and stroked his vast silky mane, and then I climbed right out the window and slid down his arched neck until I reached his big broad back. He spread his great feathery wings and reared upward, up and **up** and **UP**, into the night sky. I wound my hands in his mane and clenched my knees against his warm coat. We soared all the way up and over the moon, then swooped right down to the ocean till the surf splashed us.

We flew over villages and towns and great cities, and then back to the rolling hills of the countryside—great flocks of birds flew with us and sang for joy. I sang too, wanting to ride Pegasus forever. But the sky grew pearly gray and then rose pink and we had to fly **back** . . . **back** . . . **back**, until I saw our vacation house beneath us.

Pegasus landed lightly, and I bent and stroked his long silky mane, kissed his beautiful great head, and then clambered back through my bedroom window.

I watched as he flew to his hill and lay down again, gleaming in the early-morning sun.

I know Mom and Dad and Mark will say it was all a wonderful dream. But I have a long silky strand of hair from his mane right here, wound around and around my hand.

MICHAEL ROSEN

Children's Laureate 2007–2009

Photo © Historyworks

Poetry Belongs to Everyone

I have spent a lot of time talking about poetry—and how it belongs to everyone.

We can all read poems, make them up, and share them with other people. Or we can carry them around in our heads and say them quietly to ourselves. We may find we've got questions about them, and we can let those questions hang around in the air and see if they are important to us. We may come up with answers—or someone else might. We may find there are no answers, or several.

Poems do many different things: They make us feel sad and make us laugh. Sometimes they make a lot of sense and sometimes no sense at all! Whatever you feel about a particular poem, remember that it's a way of talking to other people. And because it's one of the ways I like best, I want to suggest one or two ideas to help you start writing poems of your own.

One way—and it's a very enjoyable way—is to play around with a word. Take any word . . .

Bobble!

Bobble.

That's a word. We can make other words using **bobble**, like **bobbly** and **bobbles**, **bobbling** and **bobbled**. And we can string some of these words together:

Bobbly Bobble bobbled.

That makes it sound like Bobble is someone, or something. Perhaps Bobble is a creature who bobbles about . . . on the water? On a trampoline? Or in some mud? What do you think?

If it was in some mud, **Bobble** would be a bit shaky. There's a word that rhymes with **bobble**: it's **wobble**.

We could say:

Bobbly Bobble bobbled.
Bobbly Bobble wobbled.

This is starting to sound like the beginning of a nursery rhyme.

Next in the rhyme, we could have two lines that rhyme with each other. And then we could finish with a line that rhymes with **wobbled** and **bobbled**. What else rhymes with these words? **Gobbled**? Maybe Bobble is sitting in the mud being greedy?

Then our two lines should be something to do with eating . . .

How about:

Bobbly Bobble bobbled.

Bobbly Bobble wobbled.

Flying slowly by

was a juicy fly,

which Bobbly Bobble gobbled.

What if, instead of **juicy**, I made up a word to describe the fly? What should that made-up word sound like? As if the fly is tired? Slow? Bad? Should it fit in with the other sounds in the poem and begin with an **f** or **fl**, perhaps? How about **flebby** or **flishy**? I like **flishy**.

 So,

Bobbly Bobble bobbled.

Bobbly Bobble wobbled.

Flying slowly by

was a flishy fly,

which Bobbly Bobble gobbled.

Do you think you could make up a poem like that?

You can start with a single word—and then play around to see what other words you can make from it. You can then see what else can rhyme with these words. And you can invent new words, and use those.

You could make your poem the same shape as mine. Or, if you preferred, you could make another shape—say, four lines, like this:

**Deep in some muddy mud
lived the great Bobbly Bobble.
When it wasn't bobbling along
it did nothing else but wobble.**

Can you see that the lines with the rhyming words are lines 2 and 4? That's another pattern you can borrow to write poems.

Another way to make poems is to daydream. Just close your eyes—or, if you don't like closing your eyes, stare at something. Give yourself about a minute of daydreaming. After that, just write down anything that came into your head.

These don't have to be sentences. Thoughts come in all shapes and sizes: single words, sounds, words that repeat themselves, things people have said to you, things you wish you had said or done.

As you write, let them tumble down onto the page.

It doesn't matter if it makes sense or not. Just let them roll out.

Now look at what you've written. Here's mine:

→ Glass. Cold. Bits of glass in the sink. Glass. Blood. ←

This is me remembering how I dropped a glass in the sink and it broke. Then—very foolishly!—I tried to pick it up and cut myself.

Another thing I can do is take the words I wrote down and make the kind of poem I call an impression: that's a word-picture. It doesn't have to be made up of "correct" sentences—it can just flow along, to give an impression of how it happened.

Glass.

Cold glass.

Slips into the sink and

shatters.

Picketty pick

my fingers pick

the bits

and there's blood

on the glass.

Cold glass.

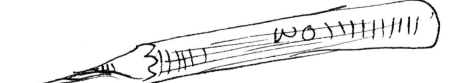

I haven't said what I was thinking or how I felt. It's just a word-picture . . . and yet, somehow the words do end up making us feel things.

Mysterious, isn't it?

So, that's three ideas for starting a poem:

- You could take a word and **play** with it.
- You could **daydream** and see what happens.
- You could try writing a **word-picture**, which doesn't say what you were thinking or feeling, but somehow or another tells us about your thoughts.

If you've written something you're proud of, you could read it out loud to someone. As you say the poem, think of each word as someone who wants to be heard and wants to be appreciated for who they are: **funny**, **sad**, **angry**, **impatient** . . . or whatever!

Best of luck with all your reading, writing, and performing.

ANTHONY BROWNE

Children's Laureate 2009–2011

The Shape Game

When my brother Michael and I were children, we invented a game we called the **Shape Game**—and I'm still playing it to this day!

The rules are very simple: the first player quickly draws any abstract shape at random—like the one shown here. The second looks at it and then transforms it into something recognizable. It can be anything: a face, a dinosaur, or a fried egg.

Trace over this shape to play the Shape Game—or draw a shape of your own!

When we were children, Michael and I thought the game was our invention, but having spoken to children all over the world, I have since discovered that they know it and play their own versions.

The wonderful thing about the Shape Game is that anyone with a little bit of imagination can join in. You don't have to be good at drawing to play and transform a shape. And you can use any materials, from basic felt-tip pens to paints, crayons, or collage.

Turn the page upside down or sideways, and take as much or as little time as you want—simply let your imagination run wild and have fun!

I once gave some of my fellow authors and illustrators—and lots of other artists and celebrities, including Emma Thompson and Ian McEwan—exactly the same shape to play with. Their imaginations led them in all sorts of different directions: they turned the shape into everything from fancy hats to enormous cliffs and all kinds of weird and wonderful creatures. I've included a few of my favorite examples here.

Although it's just a simple game, I believe the Shape Game is the perfect way to encourage everyone to use their imaginations and be creative. It encapsulates the act of creativity—inspiration is everywhere.

I have played the Shape Game in every single book I have made, and now invite you to join in and play it too.

Here is one of my first tries at the Shape Game: a little frog! Turn the page to see my next one and those of some other well-known illustrators.

Anthony Browne

Lucy Cousins

Shirley Hughes

Shirley Hughes

Nick Sharratt

JULIA DONALDSON

Children's Laureate 2011–2013

PLAYS TO READ AND TO WRITE

As an author, I have spent quite a lot of time in libraries. That's because they are some of my favorite places, and I am appalled at the way so many of them are being closed. I wanted to celebrate them, so I went on a tour from John o'Groats, in the north of Scotland, to Land's End, the southwest tip of England.

When I visit libraries, I usually act out my stories rather than just telling them, and on this particular library tour, I thought it would be a nice idea if the visiting children did some acting too. So all the classes that came to see me were asked to perform something—either to act out a favorite picture book story or to recite a poem or sing a song. There were some wonderful performances, and when there were two classes from different schools, the children really enjoyed watching one another. I find most children love acting, and I think it can be a wonderful way of learning to read fluently.

That's why I created a series of "Plays to Read" for schoolchildren. Each play has six characters, and it's fun to swap the parts around a few times and then to act out the play for the rest of the class.

One of those plays is "The Hare and the Tortoise," which is included here and is based on my favorite Aesop fable. You might like to act it out with some friends or family members.

Plays are also great fun to write. Perhaps you could try writing one based on a favorite story of your own.

Another thing you might try writing is a Word Wheel. It's really a sort of game, which I often play in my head when I'm walking along. You start by thinking of two words that go together: you might choose *sauce* and *pan*. Then you take the second word and join it up with a new word—like maybe *pancake*. That could lead to *cake stand* and so on. The idea is to see if you can eventually get back to your first word (maybe by ending up with *applesauce* or *tomato sauce*).

Happy reading! (Reading lamp / lamplight / light speed / speed reading!)

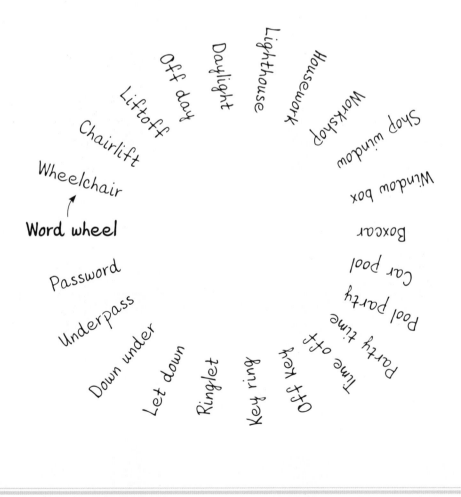

The Hare and the Tortoise

A Play for Six Characters

by

Julia Donaldson

CHARACTERS

- HARE
- TORTOISE
- DOG
- SHEEP
- COW
- HEN

DOG:	See that hare?
SHEEP:	What hare where?
HARE:	This hare here!
COW:	That hare there!
HEN:	Watch him run and hop and leap.
TORTOISE:	Does he ever go to sleep?
HARE:	How about a race? Let's see Who can run as fast as me!
DOG:	Race with you?
HEN:	You must be crazy.
SHEEP:	I'm too slow.
COW:	And I'm too lazy.
TORTOISE:	Maybe I could have a go?
DOG:	Tortoise?
SHEEP:	TORTOISE?
COW:	He's so slow.
HARE:	Ha ha ha! Hee hee hee! Tortoise wants to race with me!
HEN:	Well, I never! This is fun.
SHEEP:	Tell us where you want to run.
HARE:	Down the hill, then through the wood. Then back again?
TORTOISE:	Yes, that sounds good.
HARE:	All sit down and watch me win.
COW:	Are you ready?
HEN:	Let's begin.
DOG:	One, two, three, and OFF YOU GO!

SHEEP:	Poor old Tortoise. He's so slow.
COW:	Hare is bounding! Hopping! Leaping!
HEN:	Poor old Tortoise keeps on creeping.
TORTOISE:	Slow and steady! Slow and steady!
SHEEP:	Hare is down the hill already.
COW:	Now he's run into the wood.
DOG:	Poor old Tortoise. He's no good.
HEN:	Hare is out the other side!
SHEEP:	Poor old Tortoise!
COW:	Well, he tried.
TORTOISE:	Keep on going. Keep on going.
DOG:	Here comes Hare.
HEN:	But look: he's slowing.
TORTOISE:	One foot, two feet, three feet, four.
HARE:	This is easy! WHAT A BORE!
SHEEP:	Hare is yawning.
COW:	Hare is stopping.
DOG:	Look at him! His ears are flopping.
HEN:	Yes! And now his head is nodding.
TORTOISE:	Keep on plodding. Keep on plodding.
HARE:	I think I'll have a little nap Before I run the final lap.
SHEEP:	Hare is yawning!
COW:	Hare is sleeping!
TORTOISE:	Keep on creeping. Keep on creeping.
HEN:	Oh, my goodness — hear that snore!
TORTOISE:	One foot, two feet, three feet, four.

DOG:	Hare, wake up!
SHEEP:	No, let's not wake him.
COW:	Let's watch Tortoise overtake him!
HEN:	Good old Tortoise keeps on going.
SHEEP:	Never stopping.
COW:	Never slowing.
HEN:	Hare has been asleep all morning!
DOG:	Now he's waking, stretching, yawning.
HARE:	Where's that tortoise? Never mind. I must have left him far behind.
DOG:	Look, Hare, look! Don't sit there grinning. Look ahead and see who's winning!
SHEEP:	Tortoise is ahead of you!
HARE:	Tortoise? No, it can't be true!
COW:	Yes, it is!
HARE:	Well, goodness me! I'll soon catch up, though — wait and see.
TORTOISE:	Keep on creeping. Keep on creeping.
HEN:	Hare is hopping.
SHEEP:	Hare is leaping.
COW:	Can he do it?
DOG:	Run, Hare, run!
SHEEP:	It's too late. Just look who's won!
COW:	Poor old Hare! Just see his face!
HEN:	Good old Tortoise wins the race.

∽ The End ∾

MALORIE BLACKMAN

Children's Laureate 2013–2015

Photo © Paul Akinrinlola

Taking a Word for a Walk

One of my greatest goals has been to get more people reading and writing, especially teenagers. When you start to write—a story, a poem, a song—try taking it for a walk. This is a game you can play that's all about trying to describe things, places, and people in a fun, original way. Let's give it a try.

For example, close your eyes and think of the SEA. Is your sea calm or rough? Is it night or day, sunrise or sunset? Are you in the sea, feeling the water lapping around you, or are you standing on a pebbly beach, watching it? Are the waves gently rolling over the shore, or are they galloping across the sand?

Do you have a clear image of the sea in your mind? Good.

sea   SEA   sea   SEA

Now write down the answers to each of the following questions:

☆ What color is your sea? (And don't just say blue! Be more imaginative.)

★ What size is it?

★ What shape is it?

✪ How does it sound?

☆ How does it make you feel?
(Safe? Scared? Happy? Excited?)

★ If your sea was an animal, what animal would it be? (And don't just say a fish!)

✪ If your sea was a musical instrument, what instrument would it be?

✪ If your sea was food, what kind would it be?

☆ If your sea was a sport or a hobby, what would it be?

✪ If your sea was a vehicle or mode of transport, what would it be?

✪ If your sea was one wish, what wish would it be?

When you read out the answers to the questions above, we should get a very vivid picture of the sea you imagined. And you can use these descriptions in your writing to conjure that really clear and unique image of the sea you have in your mind for your reader.

You also need to have a really clear sense of who's telling the story: the point of view. Here's a story I wrote that was inspired by one of Aesop's fables. My version of the story is told from three different points of view and shows how we may all share the same situation, but how we see it, how we think about it, may be very different depending on who we are and our past experiences.

This is something you can try when writing your own stories and poems. Try telling a story from two totally different points of view. What is it about your characters that makes them see things differently? Is one character a lot older than the other? Are they different species? Each different character will have their own way of viewing the world. Don't forget to use that in your writing.

The Hunter and the Lion

Hunter

THE SUN BEAT DOWN like a hammer on a nail. Beads of sweat dotted my forehead, and I longed for rest, food, and shelter, not necessarily in that order. I glanced down at my friend, Lion, wondering how he stayed so calm and collected in the afternoon heat with that thick mane around his face and neck and a body covered in fur. Lion looked up at me and smiled.

I smiled back. I couldn't believe my luck. I was Hunter — by name and by nature — and yet I counted Lion as one of my good friends, perhaps my best friend. He protected me in the wild. I protected him in the towns and villages we visited. Our friendship worked.

I took a couple of swigs from the water skin slung across my back before offering some to my friend. He nodded, tilting up his head. I poured the pure, clear water into his mouth and he gulped down thirstily. Perhaps he wasn't quite as calm and collected as he appeared?

We were following the dirt path past a scattering of acacia trees when we came across a huge stone carving just outside the next village we were due to visit. And what a carving! It was of a proud hunter with a spear held high in one hand while his other grasped the mane of a lion, who cowered at his feet in terror. My eyes lit up when I saw the carving. I couldn't help my smile as I turned to Lion.

"See, my friend?" I said. "This carving proves that we humans are stronger, tougher, more fierce, and altogether the very best hunters on the planet. Much better than lions! Don't you agree?"

Unsurprisingly, Lion didn't agree at all.

Lion

ONE WARM AND SUNNY AFTERNOON, I was strolling along with my friend Hunter. My paws padded along the baked-hard ground as I thought about where my next meal might come from. I could smell zebras to the east of us, and there were at least ten wildebeests at a watering hole to the north. The zebras and wildebeests were too far away for a quick meal, so I continued walking next to Hunter. I smelled, then spied, a pied crow and her three chicks nesting in a nearby tree, but they were too small to be more than a light snack. Hardly worth my time. As we strolled along the dusty road, I swished my tail to keep the insects away. Just as I was beginning to get a little too warm, Hunter shared some of his water with me.

We were chatting about this and that when we came across a stone carving, higher and wider than a bull elephant. The carving was of a bully of a hunter with a spear in his hand. And there at his feet was a lion, struggling, fighting for his life. There was wild fear in the lion's eyes and triumph on the hunter's face. I gazed at the carving of Brother Lion and in that moment, I felt for him. I really did.

Beside me, Hunter turned, a smug smirk on his face, and said, "See, my friend? This carving proves that we humans are stronger, tougher, more fierce, and altogether the very best hunters on the planet. Much better than lions! Don't you agree?"

I drew myself up to my full height and shook my mane to make myself even bigger.

"No, I don't," I replied. "Because if we lions bothered to carve, you'd see many, many more statues of hunters under the paws of lions. Don't *you* agree?"

Unsurprisingly, Hunter didn't agree at all.

Crow

MAMA CROW AND HER CHICKS watched from their nest way up high in an acacia tree as Hunter and Lion argued.

"Caww-cawww-awkkk!" called Mama Crow. "Listen to Lion and Hunter quarrel. What a racket! Cawwkk!"

"Mama, what are Lion and Hunter arguing about?" asked her eldest, the first of her three chicks to hatch.

Mama Crow sighed. "History, my dear. They're arguing about history and who owns it."

"Surely no one owns history? Cawwkk!" said her youngest chick, who had hatched last.

"Not necessarily true, my darling," said Mama Crow. "Hunter is claiming that, because humans record history through their carvings and songs and art and books, their version of history is correct."

"And Lion doesn't agree?" asked Mama Crow's middle chick.

"No, he doesn't. Lions share their stories with each other but they don't carve or paint or write down their stories for strangers, so their version of events is very rarely—if ever—given," said Mama Crow. "Hunter is so used to his version of events that he thinks it's the only true version."

The crow family watched as Lion and Hunter's quarrel became more and more heated. It looked like they might actually come to blows at any moment.

"Are they going to still be friends when they stop arguing?" asked the eldest chick.

Mama Crow considered for a moment. "If Hunter walks on all fours and Lion walks upright, and they do so for a while, then maybe, just maybe, they will continue their journey as friends."

"But will they do that?" asked the youngest chick anxiously.

"What do you think, my chicks?" asked Mama Crow. "What do you think?"

CHRIS RIDDELL
Children's Laureate 2015–2017

MY FIVE POINT PLAN

I believe that pictures can be as effective as words in connecting people to books and libraries and one another. Here is the plan I devised to prove it.

1. **THE LAUREATE LOG:** MY DAILY PICTURE DIARY

2. WORDS NEED PICTURES

3. THE JOY OF SKETCHBOOKS

4. STAY CALM AND KEEP READING

5. THE DOODLER

1. THE LAUREATE LOG: MY DAILY PICTURE DIARY

I spend a lot of time traveling and talking and sketching. To encourage everyone—young and old!—to start drawing daily, I keep a picture diary of everything I get up to. Here are a few of my favorite entries:

2. WORDS NEED PICTURES

You can find inspiration for pictures in words and stories. "Lost in Books" is a series of mini-posters I created to celebrate the power of words to conjure up images. Open a book and you can see another place . . . or time . . . or world!

3. THE JOY OF SKETCHBOOKS

I've always loved opening a sketchbook and letting my thoughts flow across the paper. If you just start drawing, the ideas will come.

TOP TIPS FOR YOUNG Artists

1. Carry a sketchbook wherever you go and draw in it every day.

2. Remember that "drawing" is a verb, not just a noun. Drawing is a fun thing to do—don't worry about the result.

DRAWING   DRAWING

3. Don't search for a style—let a style find you. Just KEEP DRAWING!

4. Start with a doodle and see where it leads.

A doodlemouse appears on the first page of every sketchbook I start.

4. STAY CALM AND KEEP READING

Pictures can be more powerful than words when you want to get a message across. Here are some of the pictures I drew to promote the importance of libraries:

5. THE DOODLER

If you keep doodling, perhaps one day you'll be able to do it everywhere you go . . . just like me!

I, THE BOOKSELLER, WITH THE POWERS VESTED IN ME DO PRONOUNCE THAT THE BEARER OF THIS DOCUMENT SHALL BE GRANTED THE FREEDOM OF BOOKSHOP WALLS THROUGHOUT THE LAND TO DOODLE, DECORATE, OR OTHERWISE ADORN AS SAID PARTY SEES FIT

SIGNED . . . .

CHRIS RIDDELL

LAUREN CHILD

Children's Laureate 2017–2019

Photo © David Mackintosh

So Where Do You Get Your Ideas From?

For me, ideas come from everywhere: in a checkout line, from out the window, a sentence overheard, a book read, a soccer ball kicked, etc. I have been writing things and illustrating them since I was a young child. Back then, I was more interested in the drawing, but it seemed important to have a narrative to work with. As a teenager, I wrote comics in class with my friends. I liked that way of telling a story, where the images are what you read and the words are secondary, there just to add detail and help explain things more clearly.

After I left high school, I wrote a children's picture book with a friend. Surprisingly, a publisher was actually interested in it, but we were young, easily distracted, and unprepared for the work it takes to produce a finished book. Once I'd left college, I started to take things more seriously and wrote many picture book ideas, but I just couldn't seem to come up with anything authentic and original.

My ideas were rejected over and over again, and I was given a lot of criticism and advice, not all of it useful. At the time it was very tough, although looking back it was a useful experience: I had to be determined and resilient, and the time I spent struggling helped me figure out what it was I wanted to say and find my own way of saying it.

I thought back to the things I used to write when I was a child, which were always personal and often about my own family—so I wrote about a family and a middle child, a seven-year-old named Clarice Bean. Everything was told from her point of view, in her voice.

I began to write and draw at the same time, just like I had when I was a child.

I used my experiences of growing up in a busy household, remembering the funny and peculiar things that happened.

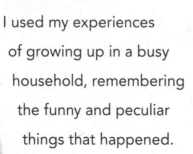

my uncle is a huncle
he says things like "gotcha baby"
and eat dirt dingbat"
he watches too many films.
He's a fireman so he wears yellow trousers he's always rescuing people from tall topling buildings which are going up in a cloud of smoke he can have you in a firemans lift before you can say 'uncle ted put me down'!!

he says he has had plenty of close shaves which is funny because he has a beard.

I paid close attention to the different ways in which people speak. We all use language in our own particular way, and I wanted to make sure my characters did too.

I gave each one
a different *font*
to illustrate their voice.

And I spent a lot of time just gazing out my window. You see many interesting things if you take the trouble to look.

Because I wasn't very good at making decisions, I started cutting my drawings out. That meant I could move things around and layer things one on top of the other, until I got the composition that worked best.

Theres this boy who lives next door he says
he likes to call over the wall
"what you doing?"
"can I-I-I play? hear me"
"I knooow you can hear me"

I think
"I wish you'd fall off"

Granny calls him
shouting boy
but I call him
a wretched nuisance.
He always wants to know
what I'm up to
and he always wants to do
what I'm doing which is
normally twirling until I
fall over

nuisance

Robert doesn't have
any ideas of his own
except copying me

I began to incorporate fabric and patterned papers, magazine cuttings, and all kinds of textures.

I love this way of working because very often something happens by accident that turns out to be the perfect solution.

I take photo-
graphs all the
time. I use some
for reference
and ideas; others
to print out to
become part of
the final collage.

There's no peace and quiet in the garden
because there's this boy who lives next door.
He likes to call over the wall.
He says,
What are you doing?
Can I-I-I play?
/knoooow you can hear me.

Everything has potential, whether to be turned into something else or simply to bring about an idea. I keep everything because I never know when I might need it.

So look around, listen to conversations, collect scraps of everything you like, and sometimes just stare into space, because that's when you'll find the best ideas will come.

Grandad calls him Shouting Boy, but I call him Robert Granger. He always wants to know what I'm up to, and he always wants to do what I'm doing, which is normally twirling until I fall over.

Robert Granger doesn't have any ideas of his own except copying me.

20 Ideas for

1. Invent a story for one of Quentin Blake's flying machines.

2. Create your own wonderful machine.

7. **Design your own bookplate.**

— ✗ —

8. PRINT OUT AND COLOR IN A BOOKPLATE FROM MY HOME LIBRARY.

3. Write a story based on a historical event or a personal memory.

4. PLAY "WHAT IF?"

5. Take a word and play with it. See if you can turn the results into a poem!

6. Make a word-picture: write only an impression of what happened.

9. Scribble down a story as fast as you can! Then read it aloud and write it again, changing anything that doesn't sound right to you.

10. Try telling a story in the style of a diary.

11. start a notebook of your favorite daydreams.

12. KEEP A DOODLE DIARY.

VISCOUNT MOLESWORTH.

Creative Projects

13. Write a play with lots of different voices.

14. Act out your play with your friends or family.

17. TAKE A WORD FOR A WALK TO DESCRIBE SOMETHING FAMILIAR — AN OBJECT, ANIMAL, OR FEELING — IN AN UNUSUAL WAY.

15. Make a Word Wheel

18. Take photographs everywhere you go — they might inspire a drawing later!

19. Start a collage collection with pieces of paper and cloth.

16. Draw a picture as if you are someone else: a famous artist, someone from history, or maybe even you when you were younger!

20. Play the Shape Game with a friend.

QUENTIN BLAKE

One of the best-loved illustrators in the world, Sir Quentin Blake became the first ever Children's Laureate in 1999. Known for his collaborations with writers such as Russell Hoban, David Walliams, and, most famously, Roald Dahl, he is also the author-illustrator of a number of classic picture books: *Mister Magnolia*, *The Green Ship*, and *Cockatoos*, to name a few. As Children's Laureate, he championed illustration and conceived the idea for the House of Illustration, the UK's only public gallery dedicated to illustration in all its forms. He also worked with 1,800 French schoolchildren to produce a book on humanitarian issues and turned his hand to an exhibit for London's National Gallery. The show included twenty-six of his favorite paintings presented in a child-friendly way. Some of the works were by classical artists, others by children's illustrators, but they all had something in common: a story to tell.

ANNE FINE

Anne Fine's best-selling books for children include *My War with Goggle-Eyes*, winner of the Carnegie Medal and the *Guardian* Children's Fiction Prize; *Flour Babies*, for which she won her second Carnegie Medal as well as the Whitbread Children's Book Award; and *Alias Madame Doubtfire*, later adapted into the film *Mrs. Doubtfire*. During her time as Children's Laureate, Anne Fine toured and campaigned to promote libraries and the importance of children's reading. In 2002, she launched My Home Library in time for World Book Day: with more than 150 designs by famous illustrators, fine artists, and cartoonists, the program's website houses a gallery of beautiful bookplates available to download for free. The project was created to encourage children across the UK to start their own home libraries and, crucially, to take pride in them. Today, fifteen years and 1.8 million downloads later, My Home Library is still going strong!

3

→ THINKING CAP

MAJOR GENERAL MORPEACEFUL

4

THE SILVER SIGNER

← FINGER MOUNTED INK WELLS

MICHAEL MORPURGO

In 1998, the idea for the Children's Laureate post sprang from a conversation between then British Poet Laureate Ted Hughes and Michael Morpurgo. Today, with more than one hundred books to his credit, Morpurgo has an unparalleled reputation as a storyteller for children. His stories are enjoyed in translation all over the world. His best-selling novel *War Horse* gave rise to the critically acclaimed stage play and successful film directed by Steven Spielberg. The project he calls his "greatest story," however, is Farms for City Children, which he founded with his wife, Clare, in 1976; the charity offers children from towns and cities across the UK the chance of a week in the countryside. During his tenure as Laureate, Michael Morpurgo toured schools to promote literature over literacy, inspiring children to rediscover the pleasure of reading and to explore their own, unique voice in their creative writing.

JACQUELINE WILSON

Possessing a deeply sensitive understanding of modern children, Dame Jacqueline Wilson is one of the UK's favorite authors, and millions of copies of her books have been sold around the world, including more than forty million in the UK alone. Her novels include *The Story of Tracy Beaker*, which was adapted into a successful UK television series, as well as *Double Act*, *Hetty Feather*, *The Lottie Project*, and *The Illustrated Mum*, all charmingly illustrated by her longtime collaborator, Nick Sharratt. As Children's Laureate, Jacqueline Wilson spearheaded a campaign to encourage parents and caregivers to read aloud to children. During her Laureateship, she toured extensively and developed the anthology *Great Books to Read Aloud* for children to share with their families, which has sold more than forty-six thousand copies since. She has continued to inspire children in their creative writing as well as their reading, launching the national Jacqueline Wilson Creative Writing Prize in 2016.

MICHAEL ROSEN

Michael Rosen is one of the most significant figures in the world of children's books. His picture book *We're Going on a Bear Hunt* has sold more than nine million copies worldwide and was adapted into a half-hour animated film. A distinguished critic, broadcaster, and lecturer, he is professor of children's literature at Goldsmiths, University of London, and has received awards for both his writing and his work in education. A key focus for his Laureateship was poetry: during his two years, he developed Perform-a-Poem, a website dedicated to performance poetry for use in schools, and worked on the anthology *Michael Rosen's A to Z: The Best Children's Poetry from Agard to Zephaniah*. He also championed humor in writing for children and in 2008 founded the Roald Dahl Funny Prize, to honor the best books for making children laugh—the first award of its kind.

ANTHONY BROWNE

Known for picture book classics such as *Gorilla*, *Voices in the Park*, and *Willy the Wimp*, Anthony Browne is among the most celebrated author-illustrators working today. Two-time winner of the Kate Greenaway Medal and three-time winner of the Kurt Maschler Award, he was the first British illustrator to receive the Hans Christian Andersen Award. As Children's Laureate, he supported the development of visual as well as verbal literacy in children. His most ambitious project during his two years was the Shape Game auction, which brought together forty-five writers, illustrators, fine artists, and celebrities to create artwork to raise money for Rainbow Trust Children's Charity and promote the importance of creativity. With contributors including Peter Blake, Axel Scheffler, Emma Thompson, and Ian McEwan, the program resulted in a new book, *Play the Shape Game*, and provided learning resources for teachers and families.

7

AXEL
SCHEFFLER ↙

JULIA THE GRUFFALO TAMER

8

THE
INCREDIBLE
NAUGHT
AND
CROSSER

JULIA DONALDSON

Julia Donaldson has written more than one hundred books for children, including the modern classics *The Gruffalo* and *The Gruffalo's Child*, both illustrated by her longtime collaborator, Axel Scheffler. Together, more than seventeen million copies of these two books have been sold worldwide. Her other projects include picture books with illustrators Lydia Monks and David Roberts, poetry anthologies, novels, songs, and plays. One of Julia Donaldson's main priorities as Laureate was celebrating performance, and during her two years, she was involved in a range of activities on this theme. They included interactive shows in schools and libraries across the UK, leading workshops for deaf children, developing an interactive website with ideas for performing picture books in the classroom, editing an anthology of classroom plays, and publishing a collection of poems to be recited by more than one voice.

MALORIE BLACKMAN

Malorie Blackman is one of the UK's most original and convincing authors for young adults. She is best known for her revolutionary Naughts and Crosses series, which examines racism in an alternate Britain, and, as a passionate advocate for the rights of children, she was also an early supporter of the #WeNeedDiverseBooksUK campaign. Her focus as Children's Laureate was to get "more people reading more," teenagers in particular. She launched a campaign to support young adult fiction around the UK, which included a new Young Adult Literature Convention (YALC), an event that is now held annually. She also created Project Remix, a competition hosted on the teenage story-sharing community Movellas designed to encourage teenagers to make their own creative work inspired by the books and stories they love.

CHRIS RIDDELL

Illustrator, cartoonist, and author Chris Riddell has won the Kate Greenaway Medal a record three times over the course of his career. Truly prolific, he has collaborated with authors such as J. K. Rowling, on the UK's illustrated edition of *The Tales of Beedle the Bard*; Paul Stewart, on their internationally best-selling Edge Chronicles series; and fellow Laureate Michael Rosen, on the award-winning anthology *A Great Big Cuddle*. He also illustrates his own stories, including the Goth Girl and Ottoline series for junior readers. As Laureate, Chris Riddell wanted to encourage children to doodle every day. To that end, he visited more than eighty schools, drew live at more than twenty events, and kept a digital log to which he uploaded a doodle daily. A staunch defender of school libraries, he also enlisted all eight former Children's Laureates to cosign an open letter demanding that the UK government investigate recent library closures.

LAUREN CHILD

Lauren Child is one of the most influential author-illustrators of her generation, her books known and loved the world over. Her Charlie and Lola picture book series was adapted into a popular animated television show, and her other characters include the wonderful Clarice Bean, Ruby Redfort, and the New Small Person. In her role as the tenth Children's Laureate, she has championed children's creativity, encouraging them to spend more time looking, listening, and making things. She believes that allowing ideas to float, collide, and connect is the most inspiring way to learn and that we should all allow our minds to be led in new directions and to be inspired—but that we need "mind space" to do so. To help nurture creativity, Lauren Child set up the Staring into Space project, which offers resources based on a selection of books that reflect creative themes, to encourage children to start their own projects.

Copyright Acknowledgments